KT-476-711

FIND OUT ABOUT

Plants

Steve Pollock

© **Steve Pollock/BBC Education 1995**

BBC Education
201 Wood Lane
London W12 7TS

ISBN 0 563 37335 0

Editor: Caroline White
Designer: Sarah Peden
Picture researcher: Helen Taylor
Educational advisers: Su Hurrell, Samina Miller
Photographer: Simon Pugh
Illustrator: Philip Dobree

With grateful thanks to:
Pascalle Matherson-Frederick, Christopher Vrahimis, Rebecca Digby

Researched photographs © Bruce Coleman Ltd (pages 17, 20 and 23), Holt Studios (page 19), Planet Earth Pictures Ltd (page 5), NHPA (pages 16 and 21)

Printed in Belgium by Proost

Contents

Most plants have a **stem**, **roots** and **leaves**.

leaves

stem

roots

Why do we eat plants?

Plants are very important food for people and other animals. They give us vitamins and minerals to keep us healthy.

We eat the root of a carrot, the leaves of a cabbage, the flowers of a cauliflower and the stem of celery. Grapes and oranges are the fruit of a plant. Grains of rice and wheat are seeds. Grains of wheat are turned into flour to make bread.

Wheat grows in fields.

The **grains** of wheat are crushed to make **flour**.

The flour is made into **bread**.

Index

What is a plant?

Most plants have three parts. They have a stem, roots and leaves. The stem holds up the plant. Below the stem are the roots. They take water from the soil. The leaves collect sunlight.

Each part helps the plant to stay alive and make food. Plants make the food that all other living things need to stay alive. They are the food factory of the world. Without them nothing else could live.

Plants come in all different **shapes** and **sizes**.

carrot   tree   cactus

This small **rose bush** has lots of thin roots that spread out under the ground.

Leeks have long straight roots.

A **radish** is a thick root. It stores food made by the plant.

What are roots?

Roots grow under the ground and take water from the soil. Plants need water to live and grow. Roots also hold the plant in the ground and stop it from falling over.

Some plants have roots that store food. Carrots and radishes are thick roots that store food.

broad bean

blotting paper

sand

Put a broad bean in a jam jar.
Water it and watch its roots grow.

carnation

Why has the **flower** changed colour?

blue food
colouring

What is a stem?

The stem carries water from the roots to the rest of the plant. It also holds the plant upright.

The stem is filled with tiny tubes. If you leave a carnation in a vase of water with some food colouring, it will change colour after a few hours. This is because the water moves up the stem and into the leaves and flower through the tiny tubes.

tulip

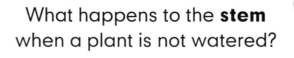

What happens to the **stem** when a plant is not watered?

flat and wide

round

Have you seen any of these
leaves? What **shape** are they?
Find some different leaves and
make your own collection.

spiky

long and thin

What are leaves?

Leaves have many different shapes but they are mostly all green. Plants use the green colour to make food from sunlight.

Inside a leaf there are tiny tubes called veins. These carry the food and water around the plant.

Use a hand lens to look at the **veins** in a leaf.

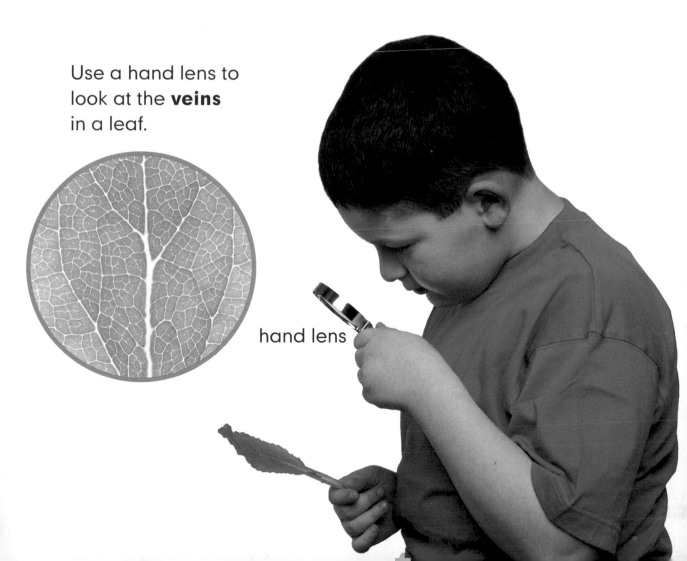

hand lens

sun

Food is made in the **leaves** from sunlight, water and air.

Sunlight shines on the **leaves**.

The water travels up the **stem** to the leaves.

The **roots** take water from the soil.

Plants need **sunlight**, **water** and **air** to make food.

Why do plants need sunlight?

Plants need sunlight to make food. They also need water and air. Plants use the food to live and grow.

When the sun begins to shine, plants begin to make food. Without sunlight plants wither and die.

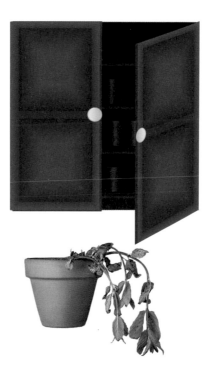

Plants grow towards the **sunlight**.

Look what happens when you grow a plant in a **dark** place!

In the middle of a **sunflower** you will find lots of small flowers. This is where sunflower **seeds** are made.

petal

sunflower seeds

What is a flower?

Flowers only grow at certain times of the year. They make the seeds that grow into new plants.

Flowers have petals, pollen and the part that turns into a seed. Pollen is often yellow and sticky, but very small flowers that grow in the grass have dry pollen. When dry pollen blows in the wind, it can give some people hay fever.

Pollen can give some people **hay fever**.
It makes them **sneeze**.

bee

pollen

Pollen sticks to the bee as it feeds on sweet nectar.

Why do insects visit flowers?

Flowers attract bees and other insects with their smells and bright colours. Many flowers also have a sweet liquid called nectar that insects like to drink.
Bees feed on the nectar, moving from flower to flower.

Pollen sticks to the bee's body on one flower, and then brushes off on another. The flower can now make a new seed.

Honeysuckle
smells sweet.

Roses have
bright colours.

avocado

apple

Which fruits have a
stone inside?
Which have lots
of **pips**?

tomato

kiwi fruit

peach

strawberry

What is fruit?

Fruit often has bright colours and smells good. It also tastes sweet and juicy. This is why people and other animals like to eat it!

Inside the fruit are the seeds made by the plant. Some fruits have a hard stone with a single seed inside. Others have several seeds called pips.

How do apples grow?

The **flowers** on an apple tree make seeds.

Fruit begins to grow around the **seeds.**

The juicy red **apples** have the seeds inside!

Dandelion seeds are scattered by the **wind**.

A dandelion flower makes lots of **seeds**. This is called a dandelion clock.

Each seed lands on the ground and grows into a new plant.

The seeds have fluffy tufts to help them fly through the air.